Norman Rockwell's AMERICAN FAMILY

Written by Beryl Frank
Designed by Steve Barber

CRESCENT BOOKS
New York

Illustrations reprinted under license from
the Estate of Norman Rockwell.

Copyright © 1989 Estate of Norman Rockwell

Photographic material courtesy of
The Norman Rockwell Museum at
Stockbridge, Stockbridge, MA

Created and manufactured by arrangement with
Ottenheimer Publishers, Inc.

Copyright © 1989 Ottenheimer Publishers, Inc.
This 1989 edition is published by Ottenheimer
Publishers, Inc. for Crescent Books,
distributed by Crown Publishers, Inc.,
225 Park Avenue South, New York, New York 10003

Printed and bound in Hong Kong.

ISBN 0-517-67898-5
h g f e d c

Library of Congress Cataloging-in-Publication Data

Rockwell, Norman, 1894–1978.
    Norman Rockwell's America : American family.
    p.   cm.
    Includes index.
    ISBN 0-517-67898-5
    1. Rockwell, Norman, 1894–1978 — Themes, motives.   2. Family in
art.   I. Title.   II. Title: American Family.
ND237.R68A4   1989
759.13—dc20

Contents

Couple in Buggy (1925)

8

Introduction

Although his work encompassed more than half a century, Norman Rockwell did not merely chronicle the times. He chronicled feelings. When he painted scenes of American family life, he portrayed them with more than just a touch of humor. He depicted American family life as a pleasant, simple way of life. Mother remained at home. Father went to work. The children enjoyed all of the problems and delights that came with growing up.

Children were often showcased in many of Rockwell's paintings. Little boys swam at the "No Swimming" hole. Little boys played baseball. Little boys went fishing and little boys watched Daddy shave. Little girls had equal time—there was the child putting her dolls to bed and the tomboy who played marbles with the boys. There was the little girl transformed into a young miss by her first prom dress.

By 1932, Rockwell was a father himself. His work reflected his own interest in family life. He had a kindly, but realistic approach to his subject, whether that subject might be Father disclosing the facts of life to son, or Mother reading bedtime stories to the little ones.

Usually, Rockwell illustrations posed one or two figures against a compatible background, and in the early days of his work, employed live models. Later in his career, he became proficient with the camera, which became a primary aid to his work. He no longer required that a model hold a pose for long periods of time. The camera captured in an instant the look that

Rockwell wanted. He was then able to make his figures appear less posed and more natural.

Norman Rockwell's work reflected the Great Depression, World War II and 1950s suburbia. He did not attempt to record the mini-skirts of the '60s, Beatlemania, or even the romance of the Kennedy family in the White House. He did, however, paint a wonderful portrait of John F. Kennedy for the Saturday Evening Post in 1963.

Each of the decades in which Rockwell painted was different. He produced the major portion of his work between 1930 and the 1970s. These decades differed considerably from one another, and in many ways. The Jitterbug was not the Twist. Flappers did not wear poodle skirts. Teens did not cuddle up in Model Ts at the drive-in. But boys and girls still went to high school proms. Father was the breadwinner. Mother baked cookies and held the fabric of family life together.

Rockwell did not update his material for the 1970s, either, although he continued to create art in that decade. Instead, his work still highlighted the ideal American family. He pointed a kindly finger at the foibles of family members in his gentle manner.

Although much of his work depicts idyllic, small-town life, Rockwell occasionally portrayed urban grime. While a picture might be titled "WALKING TO CHURCH," the path that the family takes exposes a nearby city street. The family have donned their Sunday best. As they make their way to church, the path has taken them by a seedy rooming house and the Silver Slipper Grill, where the newspaper and milk bottles still stand outside on the step. Dirt and debris cover the sidewalk. But such details are absorbed by the onlooker only upon closer inspection. They merely add color to the scene.

This family album shows children growing up in the 20s and 30s, courting and marrying in the 30s and 40s, bringing up their family in the 50s and ends with a nostalgic look at grandparents. Norman Rockwell's ability to tell a story clearly and succinctly makes his work so alive, and the stories he tells are universal.

Although his family background was English, Rockwell was American to the tip of his paint brush, as was his American family. His art had a universal yet simple quality. Doubtless, in decades to come, future generations will still smile kindly upon this great illustrator's work.

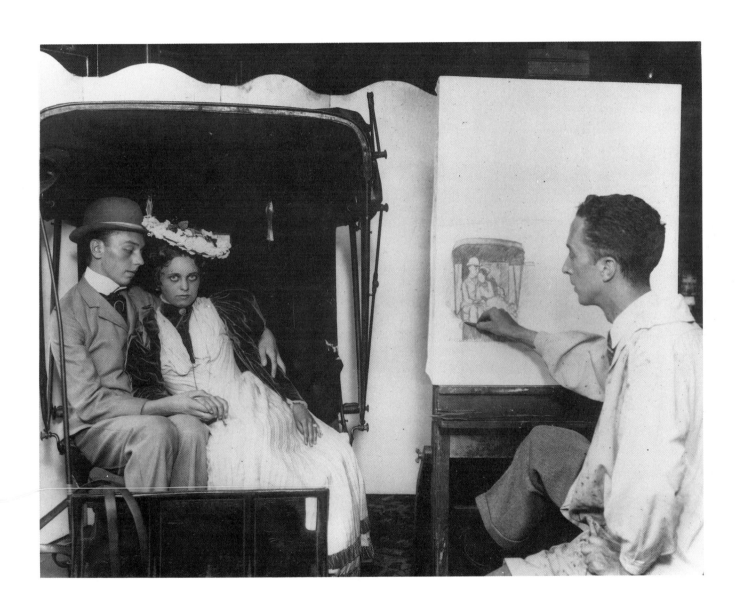

Home for Christmas (1967)

Chapter 1
Growing Up

The Family Album

Norman Rockwell paintings and illustrations are like a family photograph album. The wonderful part is that one can watch his own family in this album. Even the flavor and charm of the all-American hometown found an outlet through a Rockwell painting. Although certain details may confine a scenario to a certain time, the characters are timeless and the family remains today—along with the same happiness and charm—just as it was in all the years of the Rockwell pictures.

Family albums capture different members at various moments in their lives. This album shows Moms and Dads growing up, courting, getting married and raising their own families. It seems that in no time at all they become Grandmas and Grandpas. Stroll through the years in this album: it is sure to bring back memories of a special person or a special time. This album captures images of people we all like, and each page provides a new glimpse into what family life is all about.

A Norman Rockwell Family

"American as apple pie" is an apt expression describing Rockwell's family. The great illustrator captured the feelings of adults and children alike. His pictures reflect occasions that took place from Maine to Florida, from New York to California—indeed, all across this great country. Little boys played marbles on the farm as well as in the city. Little girls loved their dolls, and devoted mothers and fathers still tuck their little ones into bed at night.

One interpretation of a family is a group of people of common ancestry. Another might be a group of individuals living under a single roof and perhaps under one leader. Norman Rockwell did not require anyone to provide his concept of the American family; he already understood it well and portrayed it lovingly.

Rockwell's pictorial family included two parents, assorted children, adoring grandparents, and generally a dog and a cat. Grandparents always spanned the generation gap, and often served as the catalyst in Rockwell's family. Great holiday celebrations took place at the grandparents' house, and even a simple family dinner was a great treat. Great-grandparents even appear in this family album, thanks to the longevity of pioneer stock. Great-grandparents had even more stories and treasures to share.

Rural Vacation (1938)

Boy at Barber (1918)

Childhood Memories

How old should a boy be before he has his first haircut and when should girls buy their first spring bonnet by themselves? These are questions that no two mothers would answer alike. One mother may take her son to the barbershop when he is a year old, while another will cherish the curls of her son until he himself objects to them. Choosing that first bonnet all by yourself was a treat to be savored a long time, even if Mr. Terwilliger at the general store became impatient.

Little girls have always played with baby dolls. Even those girls who were devoted tomboys usually had a doll or two. Certainly, one of the most famous of all dolls flaunted golden curls that set the style for little girls throughout the United States. It was a high compliment to a little girl to be told, "You look just like Shirley Temple!"

Grocer with Girl's Bonnet (1924)

Dolls were dressed and coiffed to resemble their human counterparts. They all sported blonde curls. They all smiled broadly. Many of their costumes came directly from those worn by the little actress in her movies. One doll displayed a costume authentic right down to Civil War pantaloons!

Many a handy needlewoman created her own stylish dresses for her daughter's dolls. Lucky was the little girl whose doll's dress matched her own! The mother who had made both dresses was rewarded with a sunny smile and generous hug.

Children have always looked to their heroes throughout the gradual process of growing up. Superman and his activities as a law-abiding man of steel have provided inspiration for many a young boy trying to develop biceps. Nancy Drew inspired many a young girl to thoughts of daring.

The comics in the newspaper were also avidly read by the young people, who devoured strips from "The Dragon Lady" and "Etta Cinders" to "Joe Palooka" and "Prince Valiant."

Boy Looking Through Telescope (1922)

19

After school, on a cold winter's day, sledding from the top of the tallest hill in the neighborhood was great fun. The sound of metal runners sliding along the ice was thrilling, and an occasional spill into the snow only added to the excitement.

Four Boys on a Sled (1919)

Sing Loudly in the Sun (1937)

When spring arrived, the ever-popular game both on and off the school-yard playground was marbles. The boys played in a circle, aiming their "shooters" at those round balls of glass. Occasionally a girl was reluctantly allowed in, but for the most part, marbles was a boys' game.

Fishing and baseball filled many hours. Swimming and idle time rounded out summer days. A child's world was filled with wonder; many hours could be consumed watching an anthill.

While the little girls played with their dolls, little boys played with their puppies. Norman Rockwell depicted all sorts of dogs—usually accompanied by a little boy. Shep, Tiny, Boots, Socks, Rocky—the names were as varied as the bloodlines of the dogs. Show dogs didn't appear in a young man's life—he needed a rough-and-tumble companion, ever faithful and ever ready.

Even when the young man decided to become Charles Atlas, his faithful pet was nearby. The effort may have tested everyone else in the family, but it never seemed to bother the dog. A boy and his dog were special.

Children loved summer, winter, spring and fall, for that matter—each season brought its own special activities. A child was never without a thing to do or a friend for company.

Boy Lifting Weights (1922)

Family Entertainment

Early family entertainment was provided by family members and friends. Perhaps a musical fete was the entertainment of the day. Most of the time it was imagination alone that provided all the fun.

Folks listened to the radio frequently and they read books. Sometimes there was a live show at the movie theater. What a thrill (and scare) for the lucky fellow from the front row who was chosen as the Magician's assistant. He had tales to tell for months after that appearance.

Little boys and girls invariably anticipated story-time each evening with bated breath. Fairy tales and such classics as Mother Goose provided entertainment for the whole family when Mother read aloud before a toasty fire. Heroes and ogres continue to captivate young audiences.

Bedtime (1923)

The Magician (1916)

Family fun as presented by Norman Rockwell did not include a television set—although there were radios. The entire family listened together to such programs as "One Man's Family," "Jack Benny" and "Jack Armstrong, the All American Boy."

The family read comic strips such as "Little Orphan Annie," and "Leapin' Lizards" became a common expression. And many of the inventions that first appeared only in the comics are in use today. The space program certainly became more than a figment of the cartoonist's imagination!

School Days

Reading, writing and 'rithmetic may incorporate computer science nowadays, but feelings do not change. Summer vacations grow tedious in August, and the anticipation of a new school year sets many young hearts aflutter. New shoes, new clothes and new adventures are shared by everyone in the family. These things never seem to change. The first day of school is still an important one to children.

But one thing that did seem to change a lot was the teacher! In first grade, she was such a tall creature! But by twelfth grade, Miss Jones seemed to have shrunk considerably!

If our family album included pictures of school, it would show the change from one-room schoolhouses with slates, communal desks, inkwells and a pot-bellied stove. How tempting it was to sit behind a girl with braids reaching her waist—especially if those braids were honey yellow, and your inkwell had just been filled!

But time marches on. Long yellow braids may still be with us, but slates have been replaced by computers, calculators, and chalkboards in restful green.

Schoolteacher, Mother and Little Boy (1935)

Spectators at a Parade (1921)

Patriotism

Patriotism was important and was strongly reflected in Norman Rockwell's work. Pride in our country was the rule throughout the United States.

Such holidays as Memorial Day and the Fourth of July were cause for a family outing. Father dressed up in his starched collar and necktie and, of course, wore a suit. Mother wore a hat and the children shared in the excitement, even in their Sunday best. The subsequent informality of the 20th century did not touch the family until after Norman Rockwell died.

The Social Graces

Little boys and girls must be educated in the ways of society. Often this was easier said than done! Most young people were subjected to dancing classes anytime between the ages of ten and thirteen. Here, boys were scrupulously taught how to approach a young lady on the dance floor. Certain young ladies seemed eternally popular and were constantly

Boy Sending Dog Home (1920) 29

Dad as a Young Boy (1918)

The Wallflower (1920)

asked to dance. Perhaps the young wallflower would blossom into a comely, lovely lass, but dancing class was pure torture for her. Most of the girls towered over the little boys—who fought valiantly against getting dressed and coming in the first place!

Boys fussed every time they had to prepare for dancing class. Somehow, though, authority always prevailed. Eventually, they began to enjoy themselves, as did their fairer partners.

It was here, during the early stages of learning the social graces, where Cupid first shot many an arrow into a young heart—and love dawned on a smitten boy or girl. When it happened to both at the same time, it could begin to rival even the fun of the fishing hole with the fellows!

The little boy may have been totally involved in fishing, swimming or skating. He may not have cared about washing his hands or combing his hair. His interests were generally bound up with the fellows. He hated girls!

Mother, however, was an exception among the female race. She was too much a part of his life for him to dislike. But he had no use for his sisters, his female classmates or anyone at all of the female gender—with the possible exception of his dog. One other exception to this aversion to the female race was perhaps a classroom teacher. It was possible for a young and attractive teacher to command the reverence of some of her little boys.

Little boys and little girls soon became young men and young women. And so it naturally followed that couples fell in love—with all the trimmings. Daydreaming young men and moon-struck young women became magically transformed into an engaged couple.

Maid with Movie Magazine (1922)

The Ouija Board (1920)

Chapter II
Love and Marriage

The Magic of Romance

Palm-reading, fortune tellers and gypsies have always been popular with young lovers. The desire to know what the future holds was and continues to be a strong one. Even the age-old daisy-petal proverb—"He loves me; he loves me not"—is still recited today.

Romance and youth go hand in hand and the young are perpetually impatient to know how everything will turn out.

"Will he ask me to the dance?"

"Will he be granted leave soon?"

"Will he be true to me alone?"

Such questions were sometimes referred to the mystical Ouija Board, which many people considered to be a window to their future. Although it was only a game, people took comfort in the "answers" spelled out by the Ouija Board. People of all ages played with it and its popularity endured many years.

Love and romance are ageless, and exist in every generation. The young people depicted by Norman Rockwell are timeless and even today embody the spirit of youth. Rockwell's pictures lovingly portray the reality of the many phases of youth and romance.

And Life Goes On

When love and romance blossomed into marriage, the young couple had many things to attend to. Not least among these was planning their life together. The hopes and dreams of every couple were full of the best ideas in the world. And the whole world could tell they were meant for each other.

The wedding plans started with the marriage license. In the 1930s a marriage license cost a paltry fee, and the prospective bridegroom proudly laid out that sum after he and his bride signed the papers. Perhaps they both took a blissful minute to stare at the license that would unite their lives.

At the Altar

Who can help smiling at the stars in the young couple's eyes as they take their wedding vows together? As he places that ring on her finger, they both understand that it represents a commitment for life, and their future looks rosy to them.

All the planning that went into the wedding day shows: bridesmaids look lovely in brilliant colors, ushers and the best man look serene and handsome . . . and, of course, the bride and groom are both radiant with happiness!

Wedding fashion hasn't changed much. The long white gown is still the traditional attire for the bride—completed, in bygone years, by a pretty picture hat. Nowadays, she dons a veil of translucent illusion. But one thing will never change: every bride is ravishing on her wedding day!

Girl Reading Palm (1921)

Overhead Lovers (1936)

Immediately after the wedding reception, the newlyweds departed for their honeymoon. The bride sported the requisite suit, punctuated by a matching hat, pocketbook, gloves and shoes.

That final, frivolous gesture of bouquet-throwing has endured. The lucky girl who catches it, custom says, will be the next one to marry.

The rice thrown at the bride and groom has traditionally invoked fertility, and the pair were joyously sprinkled with it before they departed together for a week or two of paradise.

After their honeymoon, the pair settled down and made a home for themselves. When money was especially tight during the days of the Depression, it was not uncommon for the newlyweds to occupy a room in their in-laws' house until they found a place of their own to call "home."

This communal living could put many strains on the new marriage, but it also gave the young couple an opportunity to observe a long-time marriage in the works. Sometimes they left the shared household with resolve never to act like their hosts. It was a bonus when they felt they had gained insight into long-term relationships.

When the young people were lucky enough to acquire a house of their own, they had the fun of settling in together. Furniture had to be shifted around and argued about . . . and, most importantly, all those wedding presents needed to be put away!

The Gifts

The set of linen placemats that Aunt Sarah crocheted were carefully tucked away, along with the antique candlesticks that came from Aunt Jane and Uncle Ed. As was often the case, these had already passed through generations of earlier newlyweds, who wanted "the children" to enjoy them now. These items were hard to put away, and always seemed to become pretty enough, in later years, to find a very special place in the home.

At Home Together

One of the most difficult situations for the bride was hubby's interest in business. After all, her business was the marriage. He, however, had to tend to the more mundane chores in life—supporting her!

Burned toast? If it happened, it was nonetheless served ceremoniously on the new china. A tablecloth always graced the table in those early years, and the two were coiffed and shining when they greeted one another first thing in the morning.

If the bride was very lucky, she had a wringer washer—and it was considered ultra-modern if it was equipped with rubber wringers. These gadgets spewed the clothes into a waiting tub of rinse water, and the process was repeated as many times as the bride felt were required to rinse out the clothes. This modern home laundry was a vast improvement over the wash-board ritual of earlier days.

More changes were to take place in the laundry room of the home. Eventually, even the rubber wringers were entirely done away with as modern washers and dryers came into being. Clotheslines displaying an assortment of laundry became a thing of the past. But didn't those sheets smell wonderful after they had blown in a soft spring breeze?

The Breakfast Table (1930)

Fun Outdoors

Domesticity flew out the window when the young people wanted to have fun. Perhaps she had never put on a pair of ice skates before. With him as the teacher, though, there were always thrills along with the spills. Skating on an open pond or in an ice rink was a great experience for cold weather-lovers. That steaming hot chocolate afterward was the best drink ever, and it warmed the hands as love warmed the hearts.

She may not have liked the idea of hubby going fishing without her. At the same time, she did not relish the idea of sitting for hours in a boat, along with the smelly, wiggly bait, with a rod and reel waiting to feel a tug on her line.

But whether or not she wanted to go, she packed a lunch for the day on the water. Perhaps another couple could be persuaded to join the fun. And guess who caught the fish?

What happened to the fish that was caught? The men had to promise to clean them, or else the fish got tossed back into the water. If the young couples dined on the freshly-caught fish, that meal tasted like heaven to them.

The Novice Skater (1920)

43

Couple Uncrating Turkey (1921)

The First Holiday

Preparing for the first holiday dinner or that important meal for guests was a frightening prospect for the new wife. Certainly anything so big as the turkey sent by Aunt Mary and Uncle Bob was intimidating!

Somehow, the first dinner was cooked and served and the indulgent guests enjoyed it in spite of the mistakes. Rockwell's brides inevitably learned the rules of entertaining, however, just as they learned the rules for so many other aspects of family life.

The First Fight

Who actually remembers that first fight? What prompted it, anyway? Did she finally lose patience with yet another breakfast conversation consisting entirely of monosyllabic grunts from behind the newspaper? Were parents or in-laws interfering? Were the two beginning to learn of their political differences?

Man and Woman Seated Back to Back (1920)

She wept through the day and vacillated between being very angry and very frightened. He went off to work in a grumpy mood—and woe to any co-worker who inquired after the young couple's wedded bliss!

Whatever set off the first fight, the young couple did get over it. Making up was both a pleasure and a relief. There are problems in any marriage—and then, just as now, how they are faced makes all the difference. It becomes a sunnier day, even if it is raining, after a fight is resolved.

Settling Down

As the seasons passed and time went on, the young married couple began to follow their own individual inclinations. He may have taken to hiking. He gathered his gear—and the family dog—and set out for an hour or so of solitude. He probably reflected on the weather, the times and the enduring quality of his marriage. She, on the other hand, probably preferred shopping to walking. Perhaps she was an industrious bargain-hunter who always found wonderful purchases that added so much to their home.

Man Hiking with Dog (1935)

Brass Merchant (1934)

Years fly by in that chapter of life called Marriage. Those fresh-faced youngsters who fell in love were transformed into mature men and women whose love endured countless pleasures and pressures, arguments and changes throughout the years.

First of the Month (1921)

Chapter III
The Family

Dad

Dad certainly didn't start out to be a dad. He started out like his father, and his grandfather, a young boy with dreams and plans of many things. One of the things that he chose was to become a husband and father, acquiring that honored name.

He's been called by many different names throughout the years—Sir, Father, Papa, Dad, Daddy—but whatever he was called, he still had certain jobs to do. Whether he used a straight pen with an inkwell, a ball point pen, or a computer, Father had to manage the family finances.

The urban father had to contend with such items as the milk bill, the meat bill and the department store bills. In the early years, he may not have had the option of using plastic money, but there were still bills—and they had to be juggled until they could be paid. The rural father also had bills to pay. Although he may not have had the same high food bills as his urban cousin, he still had to account for such items as feed bills for the stock, clothing for the children and household necessities that he could not provide himself.

Both the fathers shared a need for medical care, transportation, gifts for birthdays and holidays, and the thousand little expenses that pop up unexpectedly. Fathers traditionally were considered the breadwinners of the family.

Mother

Mother grew up hoping and wishing for many things, just as her counterpart in Father had. Little girls of early times were expected to become wives and mothers, but many a girl harbored many, many wishes and desires that she hoped would come true. The most important, of course, was to become a wife and have a happy, healthy family.

If Father was the Rock of Gibraltar for the family and stood for strength, it was Mother who offered the creature comforts. She was the hidden strength behind Father and she lavished comfort and love upon all those who were under her care.

Mother cried when she was happy and she smiled a great deal. She cooked, baked, sewed and did all the domestic chores that kept the house running smoothly.

Dreams in the Antique Shop (1923)

51

Relatives

At the start of World War II, the family faced some big changes. 1941 was the year of saying goodbye to soldier sons and husbands: sailors and marines saluted their families as they left the homestead. Women went to work for their country.

Aunt Rosie became Rosie the Riveter in the defense plant, but she continued to have fun as well. Her work at the plant helping manufacture war goods took her away from her usual routine, but she found time to enjoy movie stars, dating and all the usual feminine pursuits.

Uncle Joe joined the Navy and left his girlfriend behind. Everyone shared the letters she received, and looked forward to the day Joe would return. As for Joe, he showed Marie's picture to anyone who came near—one crew member or another usually got trapped into listening to his ode to Marie's sterling qualities.

Rosie the Riveter (1943)   53

Sailor Dreaming of Girl Friend (1919)

54

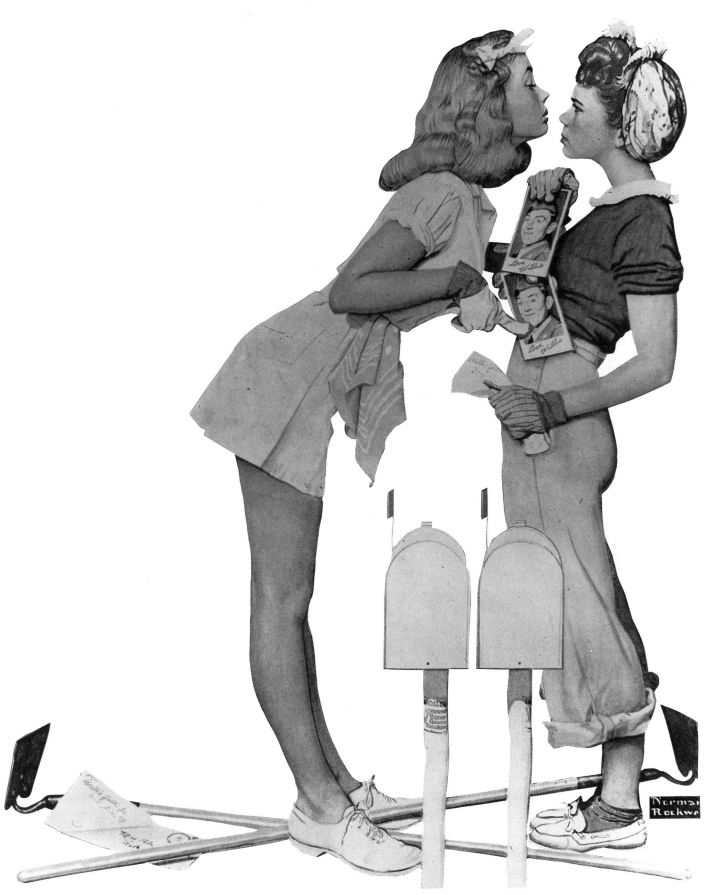

Girls with Letters (1942)   55

Saturday Night

Saturday night was Date Night. All week long the question flew: "Do you have a date yet?" The lucky ones did. The others whiled away the evening with popcorn and friends.

Younger girls and boys listened to the radio at home on Saturday nights. Radio's entire listening public clapped its hands in time to "Deep in the Heart of Texas." Everyone sang "Alexander's Ragtime Band" and swayed to the rhythm of "And the Angels Sing."

Movie magazines were popular and it was quite the thing to write to a favorite star and request an autographed photo. This activity took up time on many a Saturday night for the dateless. Celebrities and movie studios supplied glossy photographs for countless starstruck young ladies.

Woe to the young man who distributed his attentions too freely. He found himself *without* a date for Saturday night and at least two very disgruntled female friends. Two young ladies could be the best of friends until love struck. Oh my—then what rivals! Sometimes the young man lost both girls—and this was before Women's Lib!

Two Girls with Movie Star Photo (1938)

Getting Together

Holidays provided a large part of family fun. They were as much a delight to Norman Rockwell as they still are to us today. Family fun means being together. Quiet or boisterous, with large numbers of family members, or just a few, any holiday created an opportunity for a celebra-

Christmas Homecoming (1948)

tion. Certainly the happiest times for most families were the holiday get-togethers. When Christmas arrived and a loved one surprised everyone with a visit, there were hugs and kisses all around. Many occasions provided a reason for family celebrations—the usual holidays, and the special reasons a family feels like celebrating.

Freedom from Want (1943)

Do Times Change?

People say that times change—but then, people have always said that times change. Norman Rockwell's world had certain constants. One of these was to worship together at church. This was an important part of family life.

There was an air of anticipation as the family dressed and walked to church. There was joy in singing the well-known hymns and comfort in the words of the sermon—although it was usually a little too long!

Surely the wonderful dinner after church made up for the length of the sermon! Chicken with gravy and hot biscuits was a favorite. But whatever the main course was, dessert was one of the specialties. Lazy Sunday afternoons were quietly whiled away as some napped, some read and some daydreamed through the hours.

One aspect of life to deal with at any age is gossip. Many a young man or woman faced an angry family who heard from so-and-so who heard from so-and-so that Johnny or Jane supposedly misbehaved in a public place. Gossip has become the province of newspapers and magazines these days—the old-time gossipers never realized how far and wide their talents would be lauded!

But one thing has not changed: the ideal family is still a universal unit. Father is still Father, and Mother remains the hub of the wheel. The family still enjoys picnics and cookouts, and the thrill of the birth of new puppies.

There are many pages to be turned in this family photograph album by Norman Rockwell. He portrayed the greatest triumphs as well as the tiniest delights in the life of a family.

And the world goes on. The fresh-faced young couple who started our trip through this album became parents, with all the terrors and joys of family life, and we move to another aspect of this family album.

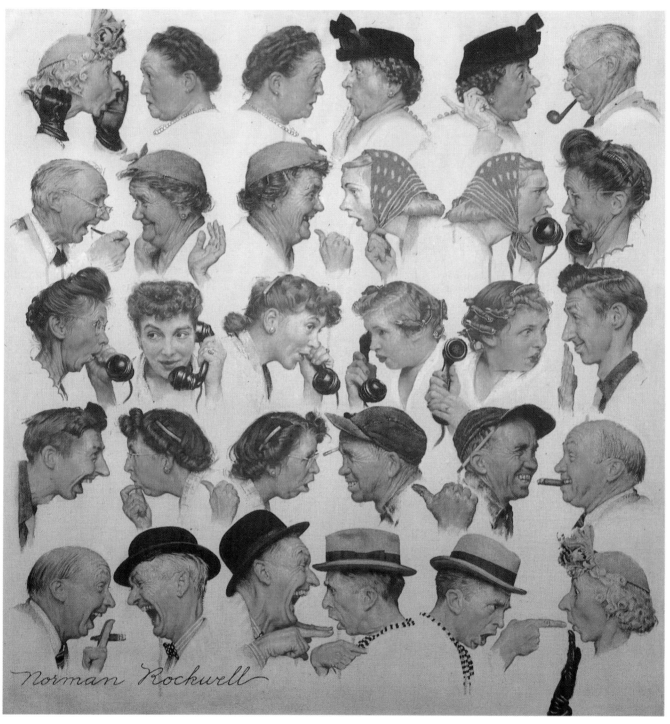

The Gossips (1948)

Becoming Parents (1950)

Chapter IV
The Children

The Next Generation

Birth is a miracle reflected in the faces of new mothers and fathers. As they gaze for the first time upon their own little bundle of life, the new parents see their future. Joy and pride are two words that always apply to new parents.

It was, after all, children that made a family what it was, and this was the common goal for the husband and wife. As soon as they could afford it—and sometimes before—the young people began the project.

It required the same nine months to create a baby that it does today, and the young parents-to-be spent many happy hours before the fireplace chatting together about clothes and names, and planning the future.

After rushing his wife to the hospital, the frantic young husband invariably spent several hours in the waiting room, pacing back and forth as his wife gave birth in the remote chambers of the hospital. Only after the baby was born was the young father told whether he had a little daughter or son. A nurse ultimately carried a tiny figure swathed in blankets out to the waiting room and said to the father—"Here's your new little baby!"

The joy of birth was a miracle to the young couple. The tiny, delicate garments tirelessly stitched by the young mother during her months in waiting were finally slipped over the new baby's little head for the trip home!

When the baby came home, the new parents had to adjust to the addition to the family. That little bundle of joy made its presence known right away.

One major adjustment was that now diapers appeared to rule their lives. One of the new mother's first jobs was to learn to keep ahead in the diaper race.

A miracle called diaper service was only one step in the new direction of the future. The disposable diaper had begun to rival the disposable paper handkerchief for a place in modern homes.

The disposable diaper signalled the end of safety pins and rubber pants for babies. At first, mothers were reluctant to use them, but many delighted new mothers were relieved to welcome disposable diapers into the lives of babies. Even hospitals began using the new disposable product in place of the cumbersome cloth diaper. Disposable became the word of the day and parents stopped at nothing in order to provide the best for the newest member of their family.

Maternity Scene (1958)

The First Six Weeks

The new baby was so tiny, so helpless . . . and so perpetually awake at night when the parents wanted to sleep! The little creature required frequent feeding, frequent changing and frequent burping. There were many sleepless nights. Mother was rarely able to nap in the afternoon—and the new Dad could only play with the baby after work. If a father didn't get home until 6:30 every evening, he didn't see much of his child—each day felt like a year to the new Daddy anxious to come home to his baby daughter or son!

Before discipline became less rigid, babies' lives were rigorously scheduled. They were fed every four hours without fail, their naps were strictly regulated, they were brought outdoors at specific times to take the air, and were generally subjected to the routine established for them.

Along came a revolutionary advancement in the world of babies. A new method advocated permitting babies to eat whenever they wanted. Discipline, in general, began to loosen up.

The universal cry from grandparents—"I never heard of such a thing!"—confused many young parents. But babies responded, and generations have since been reared according to this relaxed method.

The kindly quality of Rockwell's children, as well as that slightly pixie-ish look that made them appear so human, delighted parents. Each phase of growth from birth to adulthood, was lovingly chronicled by Norman Rockwell. He so aptly recreated the joys and tribulations of life. The joy in the evolution of the family clearly shows in his rendition of the family.

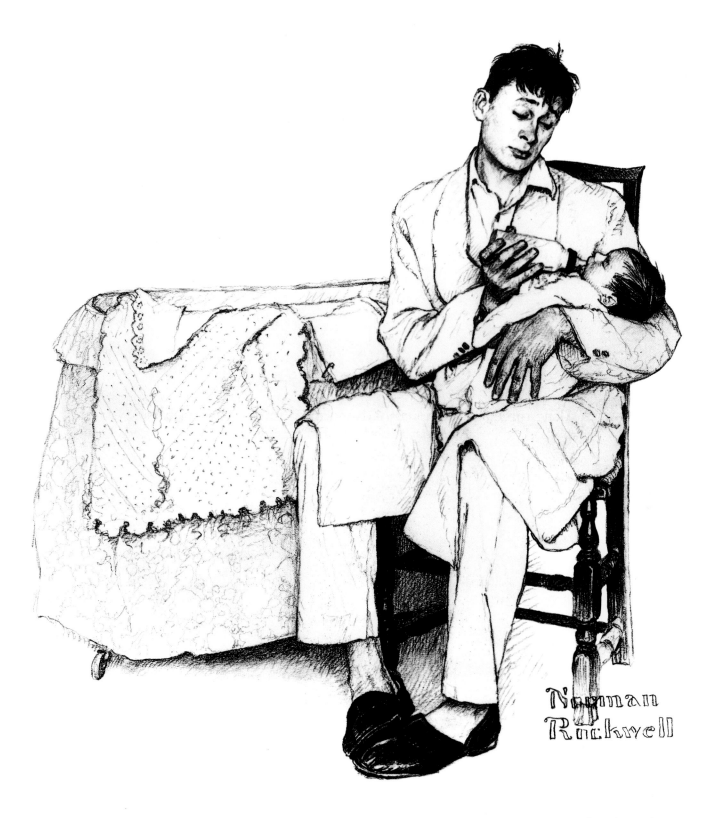

Father Feeding Infant (1957)

Family Tree (1959)

The Early Months

The new baby was cherished by everyone in the family. If a baby was the first grandchild on both sides, there was considerable rivalry among the excited in-laws as to whom the child resembled. Conversations such as these ensued:

"He looks exactly like Uncle Ed! See how his nose turns up?"

"Why, she's the very image of Aunt Jane. Jane was such a stunner—what a lucky little girl!"

"What? This baby looks just like my son did when he was a little rugrat!"

"That round head without a tuft of hair sure reminds me of Harry. What if people ask me if she is a boy?"

Everyone was convinced that the new baby looked like someone on their side of the family. The reality of the situation was very simple: no matter who the baby might resemble, he would develop into an individual with a special personality entirely his own.

Every day contained a brand-new adventure for the young parents. Each day they learned something new about their child—and as the weeks passed, they discovered that their baby would indeed not break. Confidence grew as the child matured and gained independence.

Baby Becomes a Child

As the months turned into years, the baby became "our child" and new things began to happen in the house. When the baby rolled over by herself and that first tooth clinked on the spoon, the new parents were delighted.

At first, the new baby seemed like a toy to cuddle. As Baby grew older, though, the parents could begin to communicate with a special language—the language of love. At this stage, the baby might have become attached to a particular teddy bear or doll, which was affectionately sucked on or fondled so vehemently that the object lost its identity completely. Perhaps that bear became only a limp remnant of its former splendor . . . but it was a beloved companion to the child during long, cozy nights.

The first step was taken, the first sip was maneuvered, and the first mishap endured. It was a happy day for Mommy when she could permanently put away the sterilizer and the bottles and nipples. Her baby was becoming a child.

The family routine changed and began to revolve around the child's development. Time for reading aloud was made early on. Delightful nonsense rhymes, venerable Mother Goose, and the old stand-bys were standard reading fare. New imaginary playmates were created from the pages of the books.

Some authors were soothing, some were plain fun and some stories were about animals with personalities who got into all kinds of trouble. The words in these books were easy, and were often the first words a child could read. The rhymes were fun for adults to read aloud as well as for children to hear. The illustrations had a distinct personality all their own. How many indulgent mothers put a drop of green food coloring into a bowl of scrambled eggs? How many children actually ate the green eggs? Whether the youngsters liked the eggs, they loved the books.

Baby's First Step (1958)

The Little Person

As the little person evolved, few events in the household took place without an audience. Dad was carefully observed by a captivated toddler. Even the most mundane rituals were filled with fascination for the child.

Mother was never left alone for even a moment in the kitchen. It was, after all, a child's "job" to keep her company! Whenever she made cookies or fudge, her little spectator licked the bowl. No amount of explanation could convince a child that flour was less than delicious. Of course, where cookie dough or cake icing was concerned, no explanation was needed at all!

Child on Father's Shoulders (1953) 73

Norman Rockwell's 78th Spring (1971)

Family Fun

A new car was a luxury many could not afford during the Depression. Other forms of transportation prevailed—the bicycle, the horse, and even walking. Everyone found a way to get where they wanted to go. Fortunately, everything they wanted to do was within close vicinity! Trains provided long distance transportation.

Soon, automobiles became part of the family fun and Sunday rides were popular. Families had just grown to depend on their car, when the war years put a definite crimp in traveling with scarce gasoline and rationing. Again, things returned to normal and the automobile became the main form of transportation. By the early '60s, the family considered a car essential and prices had drastically increased. Today, an automobile is considered an absolute essential for family living.

Picnics have always been popular family outings—even when the ants crawl on the table cloth. Mom traditionally unpacked the picnic basket, leaving Dad free to explore the wonders of the lake with the youngsters. Fried chicken and deviled eggs were picnic standbys, and still are.

Norman Rockwell made many things look like fun. Even planting a tree became a family affair as the men dug the hole for the new tree and Mother held the tree straight. The family watched the tree grow as the family grew. One of the first things a family member did upon returning home after a long separation was to see how much taller the tree had grown. Proud new parents upon returning to the homestead showed new babies "their" tree, and a new generation grew up keeping track of how much taller this family tree had grown.

Family pets were another constant in Norman Rockwell's art. Puppies and kittens grew up with the youngsters and became valued members of the family. Nursing a sick dog became the pet owner's responsibility, but the family comforted the youngster who suffered so with his pet.

Many things have changed since the years chronicled by Norman Rockwell. The family might watch television and video cassettes now instead of depending on the movie theatre for entertainment. We can cook in a microwave oven and wear clothing that evolved from material developed for a space suit.

Family Picnic (1962)

The New Generation

The biggest change in dolls arrived in 1959 when curvaceous fashion dolls hit the scene. Suddenly, sophistication took over. Baby dolls were growing up. Fashion dolls wore their luxurious hair in a pony tail, but it could be combed and styled according to the young "mother's" wishes.

The new attire ran the gamut from slinky evening gowns to bathing suits and sportswear. Outfits could even be purchased separately, and it was not unusual for a collection of outfits to exceed the cost of the original doll.

In 1961 glamorous boy dolls joined the fashion doll families. They also owned a lot of clothes, and were very macho long before the word was used. Soldier dolls appeared, although they were not marketed as "dolls." Little boys rivaled their sisters in collecting dolls, clothes and all the trimmings.

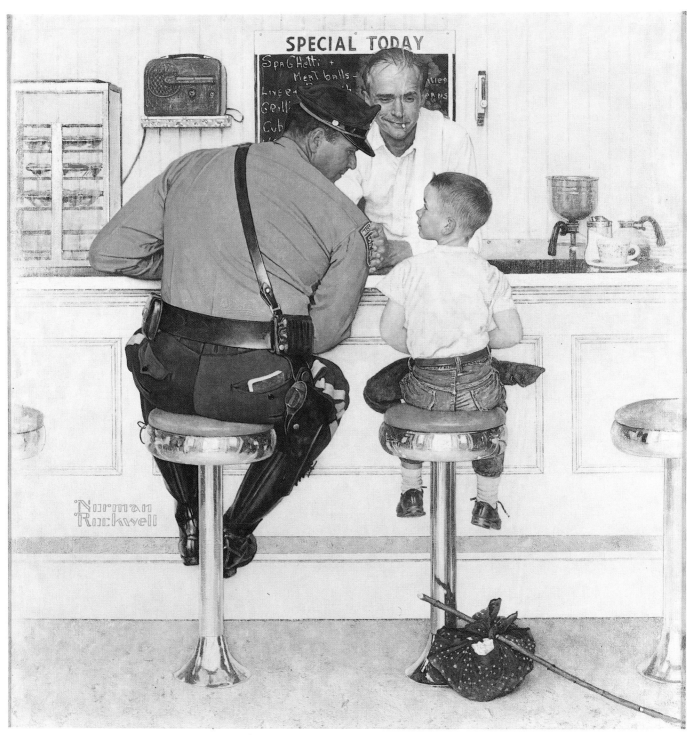

The Runaway (1958)

Who found the old wood box to use as a lemonade stand? Which entrepreneur conned Mom into relinquishing lemons, sugar and glasses for an afternoon?

Selling lemonade is a time-honored occupation for young people. Perhaps the price has increased in more recent years, but no one ever got rich by selling lemonade. But whether they made a fortune or not, the salespeople had fun—and of course they could drink for free when they got thirsty!

And who can forget telling Mom and Day you were going to run away? The little suitcase or rucksack held your treasures. Treasures of the most improbable things—but who could leave their best treasures behind? They were far more important than clean socks and underwear. And didn't someone always come up with a very good reason to stay around?

Lemonade Stand (1955)

81

Discipline

Children will be children, and some things never change. Little people get into mischief and must be taught, from an early age, how to behave. A spanking was invariably harder on the mother than on the child—and strapping six-foot fathers have been known to break out in a cold sweat at the prospect of spanking their offspring.

But the little ones learned. They said please and thank you at the proper times, and scarcely suffered the more for the effort. And as they learned, Mother and Father learned as well. The end of the day brought one of the greatest pleasures of the day—tucking everyone into bed.

Parents learned their lessons so well, that when the second child came along, they were far more relaxed and able to deal with situations. Perhaps the misdeed was punished in the same manner—but now Mom and Daddy realized that this stage would be outgrown, and a childhood error was bound to happen now and then. Which wise doctor once said that all first children ought to be born second?

Mother Spanking Child (1933)

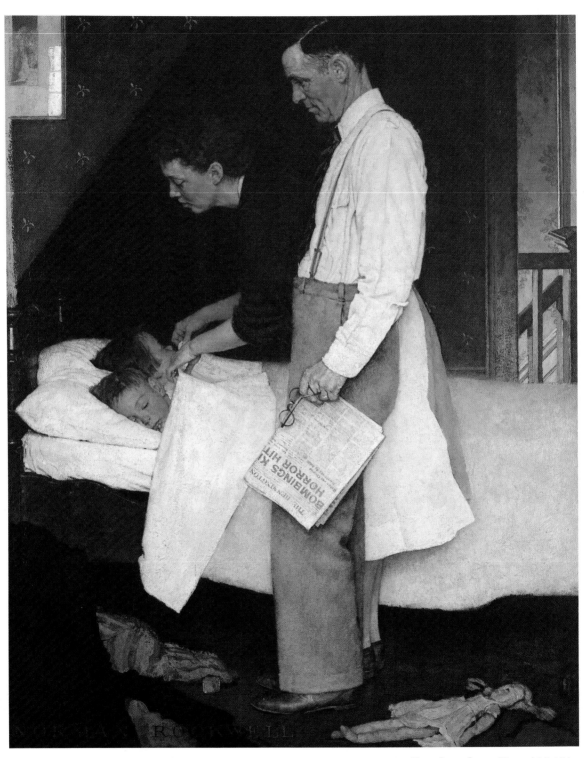

Freedom from Fear (1943)

84

The Little Girl

She did not particularly care for members of the opposite sex. Of course, she adored Father—but he was, like Mother, an exception. Little brothers were pests unless they got hurt, or were required for an afternoon of playing house. Usually, though, the little girl played with her own dolls in her own little imaginary world. She dressed up in Mother's old gowns.

She grew up hoping to become the ultimate girl—a high-school cheerleader. This gave full range to her blossoming emotions—no one can be noisier and happier than a cheerleader for the winning team. No one can be more despondent than a cheerleader for a losing team, either.

Occasionally, before romance entered her life, did she permit herself to be a tomboy. The tomboy had her day in the sun also. Maybe that shiner was acquired from running into a door jamb, or even from a real fight (much to Mother's horror and consternation). But she wore it as proudly as any boy on the block!

Whether she was a tomboy or a little paragon of femininity, that little girl woke up one day and wanted to comb her hair. She wanted to wear a fussy dress with ruffles—and she actually cleaned her fingernails. This transformation seemed to take place overnight.

It seemed only a moment later that the little boy, for the first time, began to consider the female race worthy of his attention. Cupid had aimed his arrow well—the young man became smitten by his first crush.

He put on a clean shirt, and combed his hair carefully.

If the love bug bit him during the school season, he was probably spotted lugging two sets of school books as he accompanied his sweetheart to her home.

If it was true love, the boy may have proclaimed his love for all the world to hear. He probably sent her an enormous valentine in February or offered her his very own pet frog. (At this, she very likely screamed and departed hastily—thus setting back the romance for a while!)

The girl, in turn, may have covered the inside of her notebook with his initials. But after the manner of true femininity, she waited to declare her love until he had made the first move.

They called it puppy love—and boys and girls have continued these bitter-sweet romances for generations. Mothers and fathers gently teased the young lovebirds but were always on hand to comfort them when the crush was over.

Perhaps it was during that childhood romance in elementary school that the boy and girl first became smitten with one another. Perhaps it was the high school affair that mysteriously dissolved after graduation. Definitions of puppy love vary—but however we define it, it was thrilling, frightening and very real.

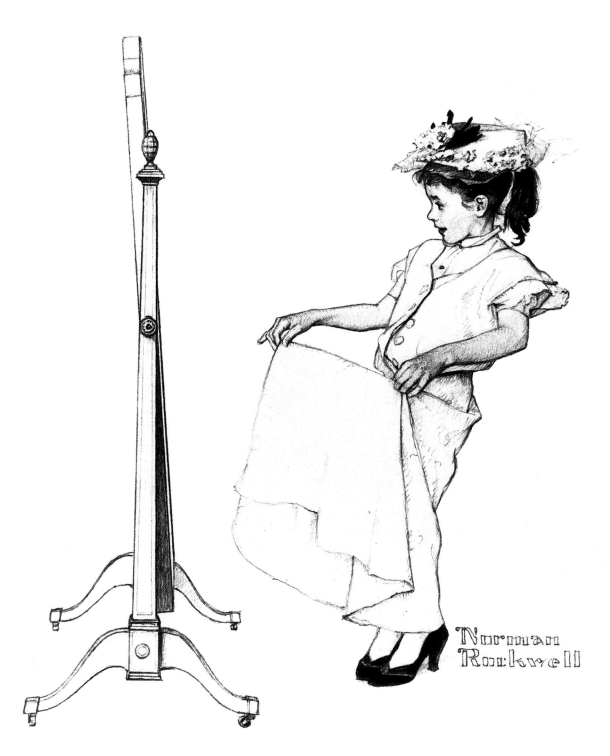

Girl in Front of Mirror (1955)

87

The Birds and the Bees

As the children grew older, their questions grew with them—and the time arrived to inform them about the facts of life. It was Father's duty to tell the boys, and Mother's to tell the girls.

First children were usually the "experiment" where this great disclosure was involved. Unless they had heard rumors from older cousins or kids at school, they had to depend on their parents for the information.

The questions arose . . . but the answers always came. The children were truly growing up. They were becoming real adults, and their parents were proud of them.

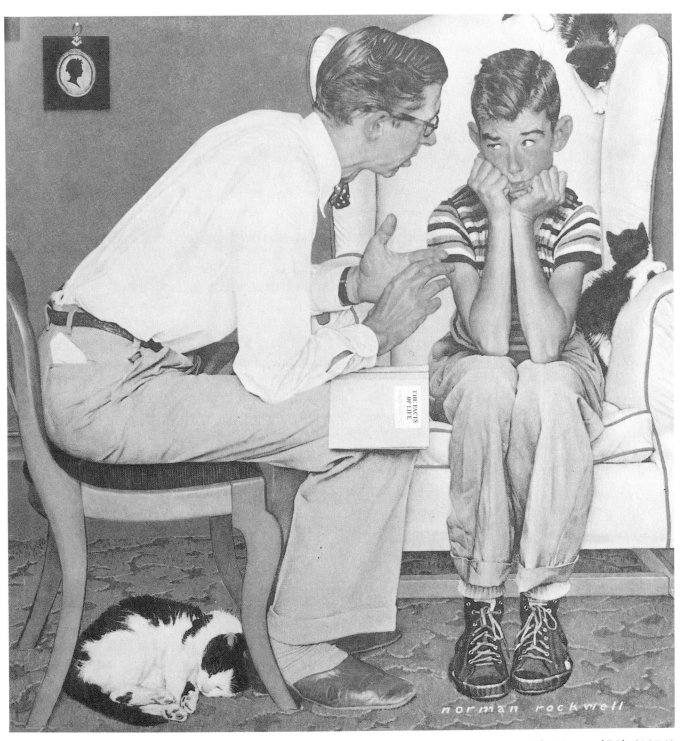

The Facts of Life (1951)

The Football Hero

All high school sports were popular, but football was the king. When the home team challenged the visiting team, everybody cheered on the players. The bleachers vibrated with lusty displays of school spirit.

Football gear transformed a young player into a brave, bold hero. Helmets and shoulder pads made a man out of any boy who donned them, and the girls trotted after their favorite local heroes in hopes of receiving a friendly smile.

Lucky was the girl who had the privilege of waiting on the field until her hero showered and changed. Then, off the two of them went to the malt shop to celebrate. Fountain sodas at the malt shop were popular—along with the ubiquitous hamburger, of course.

The opening strains of "You Gotta Be a Football Hero" were—and still are—sung by boys and girls alike. Romance and mystery continue to surround those tall, square-jawed quarterbacks.

The Recruit (1966)

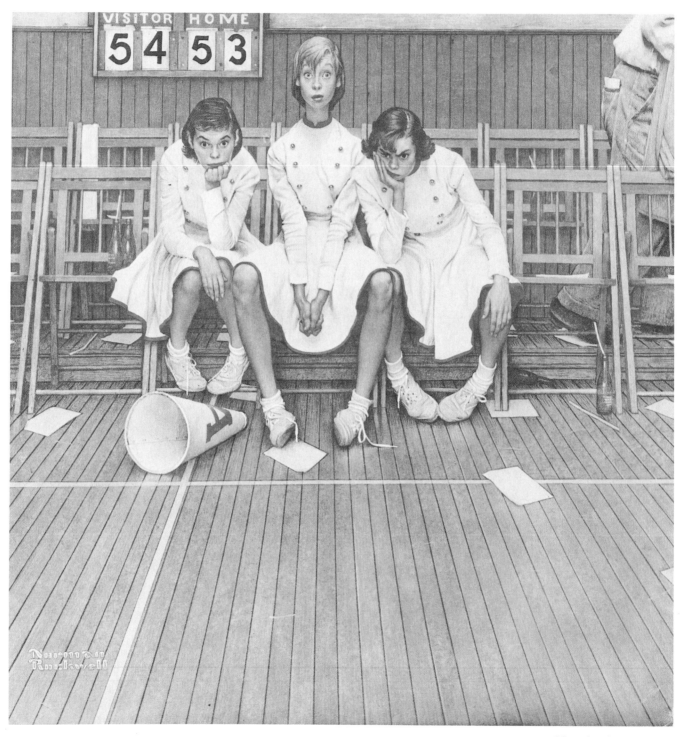

Cheerleaders (1952)

The First Formal

Who could ever forget that awesome first formal dance? Sometimes the invitations came in the mail. Sometimes a partner was arranged through some scheming by friendly mothers . . . and what joy if that partner was the heart's desire!

For the young man, it was a major decision to choose what to wear. He seemed to have sprouted inches overnight as he tried on his best suit from last year. Mother wiped away a tear or two as she realized how quickly her little boy was growing up.

Who can forget the dancing lessons that had to be taught to the music of the phonograph? Dancing school never seemed to prepare one for life's real dances. While girls seemed to have been born dancing, boys had to learn—and learning did not come naturally! Perhaps an older sister suddenly served a real purpose! Older sisters always knew how to dance to the latest music.

If there was no older sister available, sometimes Mother reminded us that she had also been young once and knew how to dance. Every now and then, Mother and Father would seize the moment and strut their own stuff to a record or two. What an amazing revelation to a young man, who had never even suspected that his parents had once been young!

For a daughter, the first formal dance called for a round of shopping sprees with Mother in search of the perfect gown. Formal did not always mean a long dress, however, short party dresses may have been the rule for the younger set.

Oh, the pride and joy that beamed from father's face when his little girl entered the parlor in all her evening splendor! This was traditionally an exciting moment for the whole family, and even little brother refrained from teasing for this very special night.

These teenage parties rollicked to the strains of live bands or, before disc jockeys came into being, phonograph records.

A party was deemed a success or a failure depending on who asked whom to dance. If a girl's current crush did indeed spend time with her, the party was a huge success in her eyes. If he flirted with a rival, however, the girl's pillow might well be wet with tears by the time she fell asleep that night. The anguish of unrequited love has never changed.

The excitement of the high school prom began with a girl's earliest glimmer of curiosity about who might escort her. Whether she hoped for the arm of Billy, Bob or John, this interim of waiting was thrilling torture!

When Billy, Bob or John finally worked up the courage to invite a young lady, the planning began for the big night. Perhaps the young man had a brand-new suit to wear to the prom, or perhaps the dance was formal and he had to be fitted for a tuxedo. Certainly he had to select the proper corsage—which entailed discreet inquiries about the color of her dress.

While he called it her "dress," she, of course, deemed it her "gown." She tried it on innumerable times before the eagerly-awaited evening finally arrived.

Prom Dress (1949)

Many a young lady asked herself, before that first formal, "Will he remember the flowers?" As for her date, this question had already been considered at length.

His mother might suggest the traditional rosebud corsage. If this was to be a very special date for him, the young man might prefer a more exotic orchid. Domestic battles have raged over the decision about which flowers to send.

When the big night arrived and the young man approached the doorstep clutching a box in his quivering hand, the girl was invariably thrilled. Perhaps the box contained only a modest flower—but, through the girl's dazzled eyes, it was perfect. If the dance was a success, the corsage was dried, placed lovingly in a scrapbook, and cherished for years to come.

How quickly that enchanted night flew by! Friends congregated at the soda fountain after the prom was over, and reflected together on the joys and woes of high school. Once again, the big scrapbook came out and the dance program was pressed between its well-thumbed pages . . . and happy was the girl who had returned home from the prom wearing her sweetheart's class ring! Whether the immediate plan included work or college, the time had come to begin to face the real world.

After the Prom (1957)

The Graduate

It seems half a breath is drawn between the first day of school and high school graduation, or so it feels to Mother and Dad! One moment they confront a scuffed-up little boy or girl without front teeth—and the next, they are snapping pictures of the same child in a cap and gown and waving a diploma!

Boy Graduate (1959)

The Newlyweds (1960)

When the graduate becomes a bride or bridegroom, yet another phase of family life has ended. This marks the beginning of a new family, and a new generation.

Becoming parents has its ups and downs, and its smiles and tears. Parenting hasn't really changed so much after all . . .

"Did you talk to the children last night?" inquires an 80-year-old mother about her 60-year-old "kids." The miracle continues, and the life cycle of Norman Rockwell's American family continues today just as it did then.

Second Holiday (1939)

Chapter V

On Becoming Grandparents

The Shape of Things

Grandparents come in all sorts of sizes and shapes. But even the very tall ones seem to have shrunk a little by the time grandchildren grow up. And very small ones always have room on their laps to cuddle little ones. No matter how big or tiny grandparents are, they adore their grandchildren. The skip in generations seems to bring about a special bond between the old and the young.

Grandfathers

Grandfathers do a lot of different things. They enjoy tossing a ball around with a toddler—and admiring the catches (and misses) the little one makes. They watch that toddler become a schoolchild, and together they cheer on their favorite team at countless sports events. Grandparents are equally delighted to behold their little granddaughter as she floats like a tiny pink cloud through her first ballet recital.

Grandpa had an elaborate morning ritual to perform, and a grandchild was always welcome to tag along and "help" him. The temperature had to be commented upon, the weather had to be predicted, the plants had to be watered (Granddad was very proficient at watering plants), the mail had to be fetched, and then thoroughly examined at his desk. Grandpa had a hundred and one responsibilities around the house!

Gramps at the Plate (1916)

As the grandchildren grow older, their conversations with grandparents become more mature. Granddad has been through it all, and can discuss football scores just as expertly as skirt lengths. "Why, your Grandma would never have been caught dead in a skirt that short! Goodness, times have changed . . ." he might muse.

If Grandpa was a fisherman, he enjoyed telling about the ones that got away. Perhaps he loved telling tales about his childhood. Winters were colder. Summers were hotter—and, even back then, it felt wonderful to take a dip in the pond with the other fellows.

Old Man in Fishing Boat (1930)

Portrait of an Old Woman (1960)

Grandmothers

If grandfathers come in lengths, grandmothers come in widths—some narrow and some wide. Grandchildren are fascinated with pictures of Grandma as a girl. It is hard to believe that she was ever anything but a grandmother.

Whatever time of the day one might arrive at Grandma's house, the door was always open. Grandma would pull down extra cups from the cupboard and pour cocoa for the newly-arrived guests. Marshmallows crowned the drinks, and the youngsters could count on a choice of laps on which to perch. Special treats were part and parcel of grandparenting.

Nothing could begin to compare with the delicious aromas wafting forth from Grandma's kitchen. Her cakes were always the fluffiest, and her cookies always tasted "extra special good." Perhaps she even kept a "secret" jar of special sweets from which any grandchild could grab a handful without Mom's permission. After all, this was one of the obligations of being a grandmother: spoiling the youngsters!

Grandparents also had a special way of telling a story that soothed the troubled spirit of a sleepy, irritable little boy or girl. Sometimes they even sang a song—and the grandchildren loved singing along.

If Grandpa stoically announced, "I don't do diapers," Grandma usually did everything. She wiped sticky fingers and picked up scattered toys—but rarely did she ever admit that she was tired. Grandparents have traditionally remained indefatigable, and their grandchildren are invariably the first, last, and very best of all.

The Name

Grandparenting started in the same place that parenting did—the hospital. Proud grandparents are led to the nursery window to admire and dote on the most beautiful baby ever born.

In Rockwell's day, the baby was not passed around from relative to relative until well after the first trip home. Grandma invariably had to wait for the doctor's permission before she could cuddle the new little addition to the family.

If choosing the baby's name was important, the names eventually given to the new grandmother and grandfather were equally important! The first grandchild generally bestowed special names when the first attempts at speech took place.

Any early word from the baby may have provided the inspiration for Grandpa's little nickname. The grandparents' names depended, of course, upon what the youngster could actually say—and the most dignified grandmother melted when she heard her child's baby call her.

Whatever they came to be called, grandparents loved and adored their grandchildren. And they loved whatever nickname they were given, because along with that nickname came a very special love.

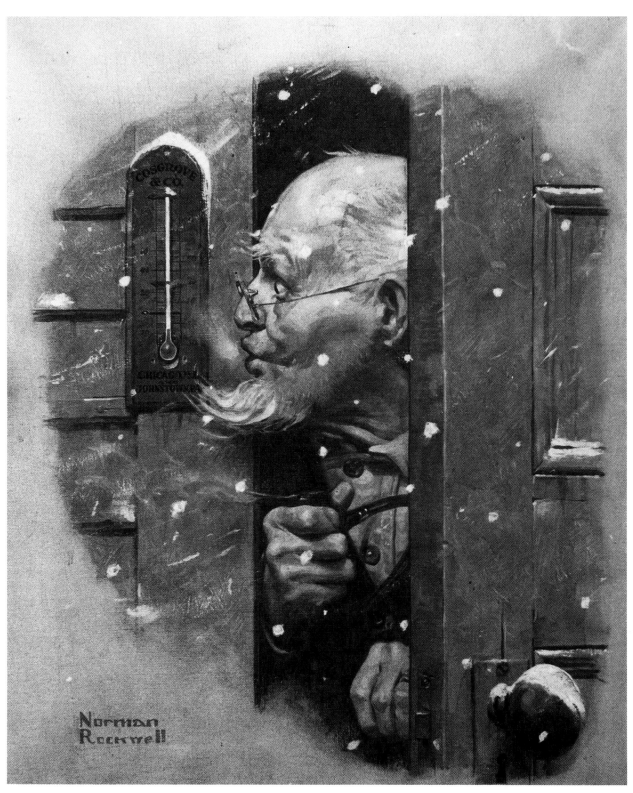

Man Reading Thermometer (1920)

Proud Moments

How proud Grandpa was when he could actually do something with his grandchild! Nothing made him beam more than a jaunt around the block to show off the baby.

"Grandpa, you'll break that hobby horse!" Grandma might taunt when she saw the two cowboys furiously galloping together. But the two laughed their way past Grandma's objections and played on.

Another shared activity was story-telling. At first, the older folks read out loud to the tots. As the little ones grew older, though, this procedure got reversed every now and then. Once the child learned to read, Grandma and Grandpa were impressed with this newly-acquired skill. No one was prouder than the audience—even if they did need to help with an occasional big word or two!

Grandfather Wheeling Baby (1962)

Grandma's Treasures

Big baby dolls got replaced with fashion dolls—but a lucky little girl had a Grandma who had saved one or two of her own dolls.

A doll collection from Grandma might include a foreign doll with a native costume and two long braids down her back. Another doll may have had a lovely ceramic face and dainty hands and feet. Her costume might be trimmed with real lace so that she looked like a creature from another time and place. The granddaughter who could look at this doll collection was very fortunate indeed.

Grandma probably told stories about many of her other dolls, too. There was the one who had her own little chaise-lounge, and the one who stood as tall as a three-year-old as well. Even little grandsons threw an occasional glance at Grandma's dolls! Dolls and fashions may change, but youngsters will always enjoy holding little friends and dressing them and pretending with them.

Lucky was the child who had a great-grandparent to visit. Great-Grandmamma remembered an even earlier time, and had such interesting stories to tell. She could also be very strict about manners, and it seems that little girls visited more often than little boys. Those teacups were just too fragile for an impatient young lad!

The Handkerchiefs (1940)

113

Twilight Days

In the 1930s, grandparents received both news and entertainment from the radio. The newspaper was thoroughly read, but every night they settled down near the radio to hear what was going on in their world. Certainly, one of the highlights of that time—and one that Grandpa surely relayed to any audience that would listen—was the great Joe Louis fight in 1938. 24-year-old Joe Louis fought Max Schmeling in a boxing rematch of only 124 seconds. Millions of fans listened to the fight on the radio, and millions heard Arthur Donovan give the countdown and declare Joe Louis the world's champion.

If you left the room for a glass of milk or a snack, you probably missed the whole fight! Boxing history was made during those two minutes—and the grandparents heard it firsthand in their own living room.

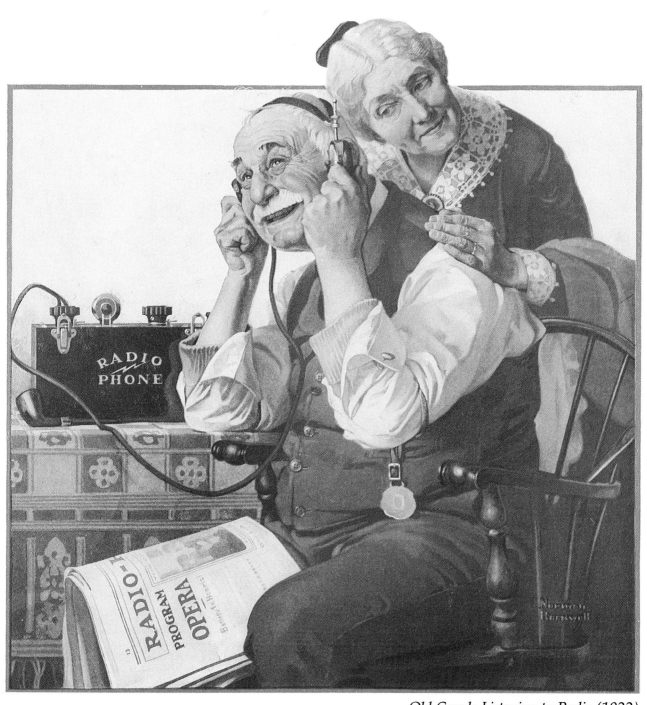

Old Couple Listening to Radio (1922)

Soldier and Girl With Letter (1919)

Memories may or may not reside in the attic, but when Grandma found an old letter written in green ink, she recalled those days when Grandpa was a World War I soldier. Grandpa always used green ink—and there were plenty of letters from him. Grandma had saved every one, and cherished those private moments when she stole up to the attic to reread them.

Perhaps Grandma unearthed an old pair of ice skates in that attic. She had worn them when she was seventeen and the boat lake had frozen. How poignantly she remembered warming her hands over an open fire and drinking hot chocolate! The skates were still sleek with elegant high tops and long laces—scarcely worse for the wear, either, after fifty years!

Was that a pair of theater tickets there, in that trunk, to the first stage show Grandma and Grandpa had attended? How they had both loved that show! Perhaps Grandma began to hum an old show tune as the memories tumbled back.

Yet another item in the attic was a pair of tiny white satin wedding shoes (Grandma was not very big when she got married). The shoes sported a distinctive platform and a very high heel, with a peculiar strap across the ankle. Regardless of the grandchildren's reactions to these oddities, Grandma still considered them the most elegant little slippers she had ever worn.

The grandchildren might not have understood Grandma's fussing and bustling about in the attic, but she was having a wonderful time digging up those memories—and the grandchildren were fascinated by the strange and wonderful things she unearthed.

Fun For All

When propriety allowed it, Grandpa shed his coat and tie and went out on the ballfield with his grandchildren. If several family members were gathered, many a Sunday afternoon was devoted to a family ball game.

Grandpa fished with a passion in the summertime, and usually had a story to tell about what fishing life was like when he was a boy. The requisite rods and reels, the old creek and the great worm-hunt stories have not really changed all that much. The thrill of catching a big one excited Grandpa and his listeners equally. And of course, Grandpa never told anyone about the naps. Sometimes they were the best part of the fishing trip.

A wry sense of humor kept a smile on Grandpa's face as he shared the secret of making snow angels with the grandchildren. Then it was on to the biggest and best snowman ever. The juvenile creator of such a snowman had plenty of advice from Grandpa and help from Grandma in procuring an old hat and pipe. Once the outdoor fun was over, Grandma had steaming mugs of cocoa ready, and the discussion turned to what life was like "when I was your age."

Grandfather and Snowman (1919)

Circuses don't change—those three rings are still full of too much to see! The animals are enchanting and the man on the flying trapeze never ceases to amaze everyone. Grandma and Grandpa might have bought a little too much cotton candy, but they had a wonderful time themselves as they watched their grandchildren enjoy the wonders of the circus world. The opportunities for snapshots for the family album during outings were countless.

One could always count on scaring Grandpa at Halloween. He could never guess who that little ghost was! And his exclamations of surprise always thrilled the child within the costume.

Perhaps Grandpa was a camera buff—and whatever camera he used, Grandpa always preserved on film the wonderful moments of grandparenthood. Albums were filled with anything from the first baby pictures to the last grandchild's wedding. Grandchildren could be sure of an ongoing record of life's special moments. Lucky was the grandchild whose Grandma wore a corsage and marched down the aisle on Grandpa's arm on that grandchild's wedding day!

Grandfather Frightened by Jack–O–Lantern (1920)

Special Love

The cycle from new-born baby to loving grandparents is one that continues without end. Norman Rockwell recognized this endlessness and captured it in his illustrations of the American family. Success, failures, and foibles are all part of this group so lovingly portrayed in the Rockwell family album.

As we turn from one page to another, we remember that behind the smiles and the sadness is one common denominator—a very special love that bonds each member of the family to the others. These characters remain timeless, and the family itself is not so very different today from Norman Rockwell's family.

Under the Mistletoe (1919)

Picture Credits: